IN CELEBRATION OF YOU

FUN ACTIVITIES TO HELP REDISCOVER YOU

BY

TAMIA DOW

Copyright © 2019 Tamia Dow

www.tamiadow.com

ISBN:9781099506222

Proceeds:
A portion of the proceeds from this book will go towards Domestic Violence and Sex Trafficking awareness education.

DEDICATION

This book is dedicated to my mom, Jeannette C. Dow.

TABLE OF CONTENTS

ACKNOWLEDGMENTS

I am thankful for:

God who carries me through this beautiful life He's blessed me with and for the path He has for me to walk to fulfill His plan for my life.

My mom, Jeannette Dow for always being my biggest cheerleader.

My father, Zellie Lee Dow Jr (deceased) who inspired me to do all that I put my mind to.

My Grandparents :
Zellie Dow (deceased)
Effie B Dow (deceased)
Sadie Coleman (deceased)
Nelson Coleman (deceased)

My clients, coaches, mentors, family, friends and random strangers that helped me create this book.

Kristen Arbour for her assistance in designing this book cover.

Everyone who purchases this book for helping me fund my mission to help people live free from violence and oppression.

INTRODUCTION

My favorite part of my client coaching calls is our time of celebrations. I love hearing the goals they have accomplished since the last time we talked. Celebrations are first and mandatory.

In my Writer's Workshops my students rave about the reflective exercises I walked them through. I share a few of these processes here. I combine these two activities.

This journal is a way to carry your celebrations with you wherever you go as a reminder of just how amazing you are. You have accomplished many great things in your life. Write them out so that you remember them and then plan how you will celebrate what life has in store for you as you move forward on your Life Path.

HOW TO USE THIS BOOK

This is your journal/reflection book. Do with it as you wish. Color in it. Doodle. Write in pencil, color pencil, crayon, marker, or stencil.

Go to a Dollar or Office Supply store and pick up the items you feel you might need to create your memory book.

This book could also be used to interview your parents or loved one to record their greatest achievements. You could buy numerous journals and make the journal unique to your mom, dad, aunt, uncle, grandmother or grandfather. You could give it as a gift to your siblings and friends for birthdays, holidays and special milestone events.

Everyone needs to celebrate.

With all the challenges of life we often forget to take time to remember, record and celebrate the many amazing things we have done and experienced. This is a great book for reflection.

I have left a lot of space for you to color in your journal, draw pictures, and create the images inspired by the questions. You can also add your own pics from your collection inside this journal.

At the back of the book you will find pages titled "Lessons Learned "and "Action Steps ". As you work through this book and get revelation and inspiration write them down on these pages to prepare you for your next steps after completing the exercises.

"There is no greater agony than bearing an untold story inside you."

Dr. Maya Angelou

WRITERS WRITE

Writers write! I encourage you to work through these writer's prompts and questions to rediscover you, victorious, accomplished and amazingly You.

Whether you do this in one sitting or over the weekend or on the plane or by a section a day to get in the habit of writing something every day, the goal is to DO IT!!!

Let's get started.

Have fun.

Write !!!

WRITE :

Follow the writing prompts throughout this book.

For the already published authors, write the title(s) of your book(s), blog(s), and magazine article(s):

Your Book (s):

_____

_____

_____

_____

_____

_____

Your Blog (s):

_____

_____

_____

_____

_____

Article (s):

_____

_____

_____

_____

_____

If you're not yet publish leave this space for later. After you have completed the rest of the questions, you can write in your Book, Blog and Article Titles/Ideas.

Write your Writer's résumé.

What have you written (whether it was published or not)?

ABOUT YOU

Who are you?

_____

_____

_____

_____

_____

Where were you born?

_____

_____

Where did you grow up?

_____

_____

_____

_____

_____

Where have you lived?

_____

_____

_____

_____

_____

What schools did you attend?

_____
_____
_____
_____
_____
_____
_____
_____
_____
_____

What sports did you play?

_____
_____
_____
_____
_____
_____
_____
_____
_____
_____

Did you have a pet?

_____

If so, how old were you?

_____

What type of pet did you have?

_____

What was his/her name?

_____

Why did you name him/her that name?

_____

_____

_____

What awards or honors have you received?

_____

_____

_____

_____

_____

_____

_____

_____

_____

Did you create a cool science project or write or act in a play?

_____

_____

_____

_____

_____

_____

_____

_____

_____

_____

Did you Travel to a cool place for spring break or summer vacation?

_____

_____

_____

_____

_____

_____

_____

_____

_____

_____

DRAW A CHILDHOOD MEMORY

Write your personal bio:

What type of jobs have you held in your life (list from high school until now)?

Write your professional bio:

TRAVEL

Where have you traveled?

Where is the coolest place you have traveled?

Why did you think it was cool ?

Where was the most expensive place you have visited?

_____
_____
_____
_____
_____
_____
_____
_____
_____
_____
_____

What was the most meaningful place you visited? Why was it significant?

_____
_____
_____
_____
_____
_____
_____
_____
_____
_____
_____

What are your travel lessons you would like to share with other travelers? (Write at least three)

MORE ABOUT YOU

What do you do with your free time?

_____

_____

_____

_____

_____

_____

_____

_____

_____

_____

_____

_____

What are your hobbies?

_____

_____

_____

_____

_____

_____

_____

_____

_____

_____

_____

_____

What are you most passionate about?

_____

_____

_____

_____

_____

_____

_____

_____

_____

What Social Causes do you support?

_____

_____

_____

_____

_____

_____

Are you actively involved in supporting these causes? If so, how?

_____

_____

_____

What are the last five books you read completely?

_____

_____

_____

_____

_____

_____

What are your top five books to recommend to your friends? Why?

_____

_____

_____

_____

_____

_____

_____

_____

_____

_____

_____

_____

What is your favorite movie? Why?

_____

_____

_____

_____

_____

_____

What is your favorite Christmas movie? Why?

_____

_____

_____

_____

_____

_____

_____

_____

_____

_____

_____

What is your favorite quote?

_____

_____

_____

_____

_____

What does this quote mean to you?

_____

_____

_____

_____

_____

_____

DEAR YOUNGER YOU

Dear Young/Little _____, **(Your name here)**

Create a love letter, a letter of encouragement to your younger self. Pick the stage of life that you really could have used your current advice. Then write yourself a letter. After you write this letter decide who you need to share these lessons with.

_____

_____

_____

_____

_____

_____

_____

_____

_____

_____

_____

_____

_____

_____

_____

_____

_____

_____

_____

_____

_____

_____

_____

Who do you need to share these life lessons with?

DEAR YOU

Create a love letter, a letter of encouragement to your current self. You, right now in your current situation. It can only be positive, inspirational and uplifting. This letter can be your "Go To" letter that you read when you are feeling low and in need of a confidence boost.

_____

_____

_____

_____

_____

_____

_____

_____

_____

_____

_____

_____

_____

_____

_____

_____

_____

_____

_____

_____

_____

_____

_____

DRAW YOUR VISION OF HAPPY

YOUR LIFE, THE MUSICAL

Create the soundtrack to your life:

What is your favorite song and why?

_____

_____

_____

_____

If you were to create a soundtrack (playlist) for your life what songs would be on it?

_____

_____

_____

_____

_____

_____

_____

_____

_____

_____

_____

_____

_____

_____

_____

_____

_____

_____

_____

_____

To help answer those questions answer these:

What were your favorite songs in high school?

_____
_____
_____
_____
_____
_____

What were your favorite songs in college?

_____
_____
_____
_____
_____

What was your favorite song during your career?

_____
_____
_____
_____
_____

What is your favorite song now?

_____
_____
_____
_____
_____

What genre of music did you listen to when you were young ?

_____
_____
_____
_____
_____
_____
_____
_____
_____

What do you listen to now?

_____
_____
_____
_____
_____
_____
_____
_____
_____
_____
_____

If it is different, why?

_____
_____
_____

_____

_____

_____

_____

_____

_____

_____

_____

_____

_____

_____

_____

What song inspires you to stand up and sing at the top of your voice (no matter who is around)?

_____

_____

_____

_____

_____

_____

_____

_____

_____

_____

_____

YOUR LIFE, THE MOVIE

If your life were a movie which actor would play you? (You can pick any actor at any stage of their career living or dead.)

_____

_____

_____

_____

_____

Why did you pick this actor?

_____

_____

_____

_____

_____

What story from your life would you open the movie with ?

_____

_____

_____

_____

_____

_____

_____

_____

_____

What other stories would you share?

_____

_____

_____

_____

_____

_____

_____

_____

_____

_____

_____

_____

_____

_____

_____

_____

_____

_____

What genre of film would your life story be?

What would be the final scene in your movie?

_____

_____

_____

_____

_____

Pick a famous person you would like to meet whether they are an actor, politician, religious figure, scientist, living, or dead and write out what you would say to them if you met them. Create a dialogue between the two of you.

What was the true message you wanted to communicate to them?

_____

_____

_____

_____

_____

If this person is still alive decide if you may want to reach out to them and share your message. (please ensure these are positive solution-based communications. Spread/Share Light not negativity)

MORE ABOUT YOU 2

DRAW YOUR VISION OF SUCCESS

Define You:

Who Do You Say You Are?

_____

_____

_____

_____

_____

_____

_____

_____

_____

_____

_____

Character traits

Circle all that applies to you. After you have circled all that applies number your top three traits. Write them in the space provided.

Honest
Bold
Courageous
Confident
Optimistic
Loyal
Conscientious
Insightful
Compassionate
Kind
Integrity
Humility
Generous
Self-control
Goal oriented
Persistent
Respectful
Responsible
Fair
Fair-minded
Adventurous
Articulate
Approachable
Clever
Cheerful
Calm

Courteous
Cooperative
Devoted
Diligent
Easy-going
Organized
Creative
Determined
Efficient
Educated
Eloquent
Energetic
Inspiring
Enthusiastic
Flexible
Focused
Friendly
Intelligence
Imaginative
Intuitive
Open-minded
Patient
Persuasive
Punctual
Resourceful
Quick learner
Technologically savvy
Relaxed
A good listener
Add your own

List Your Top Three Characteristics

1. _____
2. _____
3. _____

Go to your social media accounts and ask, "what three words would you use to describe me?" or if that seems too daunting ask "what word would you use to describe me?" Then write the words they share in this journal.

_____
_____
_____
_____
_____
_____
_____
_____
_____
_____
_____
_____
_____
_____
_____
_____

Write your Power Statement. (For example. "I believe I can do anything I put my mind to. I believe in freedom, love and peace. I believe in God.")

_____

_____

_____

_____

_____

_____

_____

_____

_____

"You are who you say you are. You are what you believe. "

Tamia Dow

I AM

I am amazing.

I am beautiful.

I am smart.

I am kind.

I am creative.

I am loved.

I am grateful.

I am powerful.

I am bold.

I am a child of the Most High God.

I am a world changer.

I am resourceful.

I am dynamic.

I am enough.

I am worthy.

I am just as I am.

The power of the words that come out of your mouth, the words you say about yourself, write about yourself, and think about yourself do affect who you are because you are listening.

Words are powerful. They can lift you up or tear you down. By the words that you are saying to yourself you are either encouraging or discouraging yourself. Which will you choose?

Write your "I am "statements. After you write your "I am "statements, say them over again and again and again until you believe the words coming out of your mouth. Say them out loud daily. Carry them with you so you can look at them when you forget just who "you are ".

This world can bombard us with negatives. We have to feed our souls and minds with positives.

Tell the world who you are and remind yourself daily.

Write your "I am" statement

YOUR SIGNATURE PHRASE/MOTTO

"I LOVE MY LIFE! "is one of my favorite phrases to say.

What does this statement mean to you?

_____

_____

_____

_____

_____

_____

_____

_____

_____

What would be your inspiring motto to yourself?

_____

_____

_____

_____

_____

_____

_____

_____

Who could you share it with?

What is your most used #hashtag in your social media post ?

Write out all #hashtags that describe you, your career and your passion

FAMILY

Your Family - Who helped make you who you are today?

_____

_____

_____

_____

_____

_____

_____

_____

_____

_____

_____

Draft a letter to your mom/dad/primary caregiver.

Complete the sentences and create a letter for your mom/dad/caregiver thanking them for all they have done for you in your lifetime. You can also draft a letter to your siblings or dear friends that are like family).

_____

_____

_____

_____

_____

_____

Share a special memory of your mom/dad/primary caregiver:

In your letter you might share:

A special memory I have of you is

_____

_____

_____

_____

_____

_____

From you I learned the importance of

_____

_____

_____

_____

_____

My coolest family memory is

_____

_____

_____

_____

_____

_____

_____

_____

_____

_____

_____

_____ **reminds me of you.**

I admire how you

_____

_____

_____

_____

_____

The best adventure we had together was

I have always wanted to tell you

I thank you for

_____

_____

_____

_____

_____

_____

_____

_____

_____

_____

_____

_____

_____

_____

_____

_____

_____

_____

Buy a greeting card, grab a notebook or an old-style letter writing pad and Write the letter.

MILITARY SERVICE

What branch were you in? What is your branch motto/slogan?

_____
_____
_____
_____
_____
_____

Where were you assigned?

What was your coolest assignment?

_____
_____
_____
_____
_____
_____

Who was your favorite person (coworker)?

_____
_____
_____
_____
_____
_____

What lessons did your military service teach you?

FREE PAGE
Write, draw, color ….

YOUR PERFECT LIFE

Describe your perfect life:

Where would you be?

_____

_____

_____

_____

_____

What would you see?

_____

_____

_____

_____

Who would be with you?

_____

_____

_____

_____

How do you spend your day?

_____

_____

_____

_____

_____

Write about your perfect day:

_____

_____

_____

_____

_____

_____

_____

_____

_____

_____

_____

_____

_____

_____

_____

_____

_____

_____

_____

_____

_____

_____

_____

_____

_____

_____

_____

Draw any images that come to mind when you think of your perfect day:

When will you start creating your perfect life?

_____

_____

_____

_____

_____

What the first step you need to do?

_____

_____

_____

_____

_____

_____

_____

_____

What is the next step?

_____

_____

_____

_____

_____

_____

_____

When will you do (implement) these steps?

_____

_____

_____

Who will you reach out to in order to hold yourself accountable in completing these steps?

_____

_____

_____

How much is this dream life worth to you?

_____

_____

_____

_____

_____

_____

_____

_____

_____

How will you feel when you have achieved it?

_____

_____

_____

_____

_____

_____

_____

_____

Why is this lifestyle important to you?

_____

_____

_____

_____

_____

_____

_____

_____

Who can you help when you achieved your perfect life?

_____
_____
_____
_____
_____

What are you waiting for?

_____
_____
_____
_____
_____

The world needs you at your best.
Step Up.
Step Out.
Defeat Fear and
DO IT!!!

Then contact me and we will CELEBRATE YOU !!!

THE INEVITABLE

BREAKING NEWS:

10 out of 10 people will die. I know this is a shock to you yet it's a fact. None of us are getting out of here alive.

How will you be remembered? What will people say about you? Who knows your life story?

I encourage you to use the questions asked and the ideas promoted by this book to write your own Eulogy.

Save your loved ones the pain of writing your Eulogy while they are grieving your loss. This is one of the kindest things you can do for your family. Writing your own Eulogy and having a trust and will in place to give your family your final instructions will ease the transition of your passing.

Your desires for all that you have accumulated in your lifetime will be spelled out in your trust and will.

Tomorrow is not promised to any of us.

You cannot take it with you. There are no U-Hauls allowed in the funeral procession to the cemetery and it is a common fact that many families are torn apart over issues arising from a loved one's passing without final instructions in place.

YOUR EULOGY

When someone passes away, we often hold a memorial service reflecting on their life. This process celebrates their life, what they have done, who they have loved, where they have served and what they mean to us (the person writing the Eulogy).

Often time it is a surviving spouse, child, grandchild or sibling of the deceased left with this sad activity. Since we do not often share every aspect of our life with our family members, they may miss some important information about the life we lived.

Make your passing easier on your loved one:

Write your Eulogy (celebrate Your Life)

_____

_____

_____

_____

_____

_____

_____

_____

_____

_____

_____

_____

_____

_____

Write out your will (this is your last words to loved ones in which you can designate property and resources letting your heirs know your final wishes for your belongings).

_____
_____
_____
_____
_____
_____
_____
_____
_____
_____
_____
_____
_____
_____
_____
_____
_____
_____
_____
_____
_____
_____
_____
_____
_____
_____
_____

_____

_____

_____

_____

_____

_____

_____

_____

_____

_____

DISCLAIMER: You may want to contact an Estate Attorney to assist you in preparing a legal will, trust and final instructions paper. This is just a writing exercise to get you to think about "end of life "issues while you are still able to make them. This is Not legal advice.

EXTRA PAGES

These extra pages are to be used to expand on any of the questions from this book that inspired a longer response than the space provided.

CONGRATULATIONS

Congratulations you have completed this workbook.

Will you expand on this experience and create a book, talk, or training to share your life lessons?

What will you do with all you have poured into this journal?

_____

_____

_____

_____

_____

_____

_____

_____

_____

_____

_____

_____

_____

_____

_____

_____

_____

_____

_____

_____
_____
_____
_____
_____
_____
_____
_____
_____
_____
_____
_____
_____
_____
_____
_____
_____

What is next for you ?

_____
_____
_____

LESSONS LEARNED (during this process)

ACTION STEPS (from this process)

MESSAGE FROM THE AUTHOR:

Whenever you start to think you cannot do something pull out this journal and remind yourself of all that you have accomplished.

You are amazing. You have done great things. You will do even greater things once you put your mind to it. Focus.

Follow
One
Course
Until
Successful

Go back to the "Writers Write" section and revisit Books, Blogs and Articles ideas that may have been sparked by your answers in this book.

Look at the notes you have written throughout this book and in the "Action Steps" and "Lessons Learned" sections. Review these notes daily and

TAKE ACTION!!!

AUTHOR'S BIO

"She asks the right questions. "

Tamia Dow has over 25 years of police experience which includes military and civilian law enforcement training. She a veteran of the US Army. She holds a Bachelor's Degree in Criminal Justice from The University of Nevada, Las Vegas and is a Master Graduate of Rapport Leadership Institute.

Tamia is a retired Las Vegas Metropolitan Police Department Domestic Violence Detective (DV). She is an International Speaker and Trainer. She trains citizens, community leaders, organizations and law enforcement officers locally and internationally in the area of Human (Labor and Sex) Trafficking, Domestic Violence, Leadership and Creative Writing. She is a certified John Maxwell Equip Leadership Instructor and a former Dale Carnegie Trainer.

Tamia is an Award Winning International Best-Selling Author with eleven completed books and five current book projects. As a Book Coach she has helped over one hundred authors recognize the accomplishment of being a published author.

Tamia conducts Writing Workshops. She has a signature workshop titled "Your Book As Your Business Card "which she conducts for the Senior Core Of Retired Executives (SCORE) in Las Vegas.

She also offers her "Writers Write" workshops which she presents worldwide.

Tamia graduated from ICLV's Kairos School of Ministry in 2011 and is an ordained minister currently holding the title of Chaplain.

Tamia believes everyone has the right to live a life free from violence and oppression. This is her life mission.

While working as a Domestic Violence Detective she encountered victims of sex trafficking who had been misidentified as DV victims. She now actively works to assist victims and increase awareness.

She's partnered with many local Human Trafficking nonprofits to help in outreaches and awareness campaigns.

She works with Be A Voice (BeAVoiceNow.com) and is the Training Coordinator of their Family Empowerment Summits. She's facilitates the Family Education portion of their annual "For The Sake of Our City" Walk and Community Outreach.

She was trained by and assisted F.R.E.E. International (FREEInternational.org) and Nevada Child Seekers with their Big Search mission to locate missing and exploited children.

Tamia has been a part of the Southern Nevada Human Trafficking Task Force since her time on

LVMPD. While still a member of Metro she participated in a weekly prayer group for Human Trafficking Eradication hosted by the International Church of Las Vegas (ICLV) her home church.

She also trained a large team of advocates as part of Dream with SJ, a local outreach to the working girls which was headed by Sex Trafficking Survivor Mrs. Sara Jane Vegas.

Prior to working with Sara Jane, Tamia worked with Love Remembers which was a community education and outreach ministry headed up by a survivor of Sex Trafficking - Jodee. Jodee continues to minister nationally sharing her story of captivity, escape and advocacy.

Tamia is also an Award-Winning Filmmaker and Actress. She has written, directed, produced and starred in two short films on the subject of Domestic Violence and Human Trafficking with two more in pre-production right now.

Tamia host an online talk show called "Tamia Talks Books" which can be found on her You Tube Channel "Tamia Dow TV Online ".

Since retiring Tamia has been traveling around the world learning about the challenges facing women and children worldwide. She has presented Awareness training throughout the U.S., in Bangladesh, Canada, Curacao, Russia, Uganda and Kenya.

She is actively involved in increasing the awareness of violence and control used to limit the freedoms of vulnerable people.

In 2014 Tamia gathered together many Southern Nevada based Human Trafficking Advocates and nonprofits (NGOs) and put on an informational training for Law Enforcement Professionals about "Human Trafficking, How to recognize and assist victims ". The training was attended by officers from the US, Canada, Africa and the U.K.

Tamia was recognized by Cambridge Who's Who as professional of the year representing law-enforcement for the year 2011 to 2012.

At her retirement ceremony a great honor was bestowed on Tamia when the Nevada Governor, Brian Sandoval proclaimed February 1, 2012 as a day in honor of Tamia Dow in the state of Nevada to recognize her service to the community.

In addition, The Clark County Commission (Nevada) proclaimed February 2, 2012 as a day in her honor.

Tamia continues to give back to the community she serves by conducting educational trainings. Her heart virtues are justice, education and empowerment.

Cop, Coach, Chaplain, Creative.

Tamia is available to present your Keynote, and/or conduct breakout sessions and training at your meeting or conference. It is her pleasure to tailor her presentation to your organization's needs.

Tamia can be reached at Chaplain Dow on Twitter, Facebook, and Instagram or
Coachtamia@gmail.com
www.tamiadow.com

WORK WITH COACH TAMIA

Thank you for completing the questions in this journal. If you would like to talk about your answers or to pursue sharing your story and life lessons with the world, please contact me at coachtamia@gmail.com.

"Use your life experiences to help, inspire and bless others."
Tamia Dow

There is significance in every story you shared in this journal because it is your unique experience. There may have been many other people who were with you on the journey you shared yet your story is uniquely yours. You are You-niquely You!

You have experienced all you have experienced for such a time as this. Help someone else see how you made it through. Spread hope. Show faith. Let's change the world with your story.

PROGRAMS OFFERED BY COACH TAMIA

Tamia conducts webinars, workshops, trainings, keynotes and retreats tailored specifically to you or your groups needs. She can provide an overview (like this book) or a deep dive (which you will see in her next book) that aids the participant in unlocking the greatness within and realizing how they can use their life to help others and change the world.

Tamia@incelebrationofyou.com
www.incelebrationofyou.com

THANK YOU

Thank you for purchasing this book. I hope you enjoyed it and it inspired you.

Your Feedback is appreciated.

What did you enjoy?

_____

_____

_____

What was the hardest exercise?

_____

_____

_____

What else would you like to see in this journal?

_____

_____

_____

How would you improve upon this journal?

_____

_____

_____

Please post your reviews of this book on Amazon. Also follow this book on our Facebook pages "In Celebration Of You "and "Leave A Literal Life Legacy."

Again Thank you.

Made in the USA
San Bernardino, CA
02 June 2019